YOUR SONS

AND DAUGHTERS

YOUR SONS AND DAUGHTERS

Paedocommunion,
the Gospel,
and the Church

PETER J. LEITHART

DEDICATION

This booklet is dedicated to our ninth granddaughter, Georgia Mae Elizabeth, fifth child of Sheffield and Laura Leithart. Georgia and her lively older sister, Ellie, form a neat chiastic inclusio around three lively brothers. Jesus washed Georgia for His feast at her baptism, and by the time this booklet is published she'll likely have her first taste of His banquet. I pray Georgia will remain a guest at the Lamb's marriage feast throughout her life, and through the ages of ages yet to come.

Your Sons and Daughters
By Peter J. Leithart

Copyright © 2025 Peter J. Leithart

An earlier version of these essays were published in *Credenda/Agenda,* 18:1.

Athanasius Press
715 Cypress Street
West Monroe, Louisiana, 71291
www.athanasiuspress.org

Cover design and typesetting: Rachel Rosales

ISBN: 978-1-957726-23-6

Printed in the United States of America.

CONTENTS

ACKNOWLEDGMENTS

This essay was first published in *Credenda/Agenda* magazine in the early 2000s. I'm grateful to Douglas Wilson for publishing that essay, and also to Zach Parker and his team at Athanasius Press for their willingness to put the essay into this more permanent form.

CHAPTER 1

The Right Question

Should young children receive the Lord's Supper? Should we practice paedo-communion?

Before we address the question of paedocommunion, we must specify both *what* the question is and *what sort of* question it is. First, *what* is the question of paedocommunion? It is not in essence a question about the age of admission to the Lord's table. Some who do not adopt the paedocommunion position would admit toddlers as young as a year-and-a-half. If, hypothetically, some means were invented to gauge the level of "discernment" in infants, and children who registered a "6" were admitted to the table, that practice still would not constitute paedocommunion. Nor is it a question about force-feeding bread and wine to newborns; though some churches give the elements to newly baptized infants, no Reformed advocate of paedocommunion, to my knowledge, has argued for this practice. Most Reformed theologians are content to wait until the child is able to eat solid food before he begins to participate in the Supper.

The specific practical question is, Does baptism initiate the baptized to the Lord's table, so that all who are baptized have a right to the meal? Paedocommunion advocates, for all their differences, answer in the affirmative. Nothing more than the rite of water baptism is required for a person to have access to the Lord's table. Opponents of paedocommunion answer in the negative. Something *more* is required—some level of understanding, a degree of spiritual discernment, a conversion experience, and some test for the church to assess these attainments.

Second, and more fundamentally, what *sort of* question is this? If it were a question about the admission requirements to the church's ritual meal, then the question might be answered by straightforwardly applying a rule. If we focus narrowly on the question of who partakes when, we could admit children without adjusting any other doctrines or practices of the church. If it is only a matter of adding a few names to the guest list, then why is paedocommunion so strindently opposed by some within the Reformed world?

Paedocommunion is not *only* about admission requirements narrowly considered, but, like paedobaptism, is linked with a whole range of theological and liturgical issues. It not only affects our understanding of the nature of Supper, but our convictions about the church, baptism, and, most broadly, the character of the salvation that Christ has achieved in the world. The gospel is not directly at stake in the paedocommunion debate. Opponents of paedocommunion honestly and sincerely proclaim the gospel of grace, and I am grateful to God that they do. Still, the ecclesial and theological shape the gospel takes correlates significantly with positions on paedocommunion, and the coherence between the gospel and the church's practice is at the heart of this debate. The stakes are not so high as they were when Luther protested indulgences and the myriad idolatries of the late medieval church. But the stakes *are* high, very high.

At the risk of oversimplification (and provocation), I briefly pose the options on these wider issues:

- Is the Supper an ordinance of the church (paedocommunion), or is it an ordinance for some segment of the church (antipaedocommunion)?[1]

---

1. I apologize for the clumsy terminology, but have been unable to come up with anything better. I toyed with the idea of using neutral terms – e.g., call advocates of paedocommunion "Bob" and opponents "Henry." But that usage would have paid too high a price in clarity, not to mention seriousness.

- Is the church the family of God
  simpliciter (paedocommunion), or
  is the church divided between those
  who are full members of the family
  and those who are partial members
  or strangers (antipaedocommunion)?

- Did Jesus die and rise again to form
  a new Israel (paedocommunion), or
  did He die and rise again to form a
  community with a quite different
  make-up from Israel (antipaedocommunion)?

- Did Jesus die and rise again to form
  the new human race (paedocommunion), or did He die and rise
  again to form a fellowship of the
  spiritually mature (antipaedocommunion)?

- Does baptism admit the baptized into the covenant or symbolize his prior inclusion in the covenant (paedocommunion), or does baptism merely express a hope that the baptized one day will enter the covenant in some other fashion (antipaedocommunion)?

- Does the covenant have an inherently historical/institutional character (paedocommunion), or is it an invisible reality (antipaedocommunion)?

- Does grace restore and glorify nature (paedocommunion), or does grace cancel nature or elevate beyond nature (antipaedocommunion)?

- Does faith require conscious and articulable belief (antipaedocommunion) or is faith something of which infants are capable (paedocommunion)?

Like many theological issues, paedocommunion also poses the question of the relative weight of Scripture and tradition. The question is *not* what the Reformed tradition has taught on this issue; I concede that very few Reformed theologians have advocated paedocommunion. Nor is the question about Jewish custom, which opponents of paedocommunion often cite. (Why should Christians care what the Talmud says?) The issue is what *Scripture* teaches, and if we find that our tradition is out of accord with Scripture, we must simply obey God rather than men, even if they are our honored fathers in the faith.

In the following parts of this essay, I focus on the ecclesiological issues raised by paedocommunion, which are simultaneously questions about the nature of the covenant, the continuity of Old and New, about salvation, and the gospel. Throughout, I am guided by an underlying assumption that *the sacraments manifest the nature of the church.* For centuries, sacramental theology in the Reformed and in other traditions has often focused narrowly on the effect of sacraments on individual recipients, and as a result, both the theology and practice of the sacraments have been horribly distorted. We should, in addition and even primarily, consider sacraments in an ecclesial context. The question should not only be what a particular rite does to *me*, but also what this ritual tells me about the *community* that celebrates it.

According to Paul's teaching, the Lord's Supper embodies the nature of the church as a unified community. Because we partake of one loaf, we are one body (1 Corinthians 10:16), and because partaking of the bread and cup is a communion in Christ, it commits us to avoiding communion with demons and idols. The Lord's Supper ritually declares that the church is one, and that this united community is separated from the world. This is why, according to Paul, the Corinthians were not actually performing the Lord's Supper (1 Corinthians 11:20).

From Paul's perspective, the Supper and its practice provide a criterion for measuring and judging the church's faithfulness to her called and her Lord. Conversely, the New Testament's teaching concerning the church provides a criterion for assessing our sacramental life. The Supper is a ritual expression of our confession that the church is One, Holy, Catholic, and Apostolic. We should ask both, "Does the church's life measure up with what we say about ourselves at the table?" and "Is what we confess about the church manifest at the table?"

Paul's sacramental reasoning can be extended in many directions. We know, for instance, that the church is a body in which divisions of Jew and Gentile, slave and free, male and female have been dissolved (Galatians 3:28), and Paul severely rebuked Peter when his table fellowship failed to line up with this ecclesial reality (Galatians 2:11–21). A church that refuses bread and wine to blacks, or to whites, or to Asians, is lying about both the church and the Supper. More pointedly: Paul says that the church is a community where the weakest and most unseemly are welcomed (1 Corinthians 12:22–26). Does the Baptist refusal to baptize infants give ritual expression to *that* kind of church, or does it instead imply that the church welcomes only the smart and the strong?[2]

At the same time, the sacraments must express what the church proclaims in the gospel. This might be approached from various directions. That Jesus broke down the dividing wall between Jews and Gentiles is part of the gospel, and so the Supper expresses the gospel when it welcomes Christians from every tribe and

---

2. I am not suggesting that Baptists are unmerciful toward the weak. Many Baptist churches put paedobaptists to shame in this regard. I am asking whether Baptist baptism tells us the truth about the church.

tongue and nation. The gospel announces that God has initiated a new creation in and through Jesus, and our practices and theology of the Supper must express the scope of that announcement. The gospel proclaims the grace of God to sinners who have no ability to crawl their way back to Him, and the way we think about and perform the Supper must be consistent with that. According to Luther, the Supper *is* the gospel, for in it our heavenly Father offers His Son to us through the Spirit for our life; the Supper is first and last God's *gift*, God's gift of *Himself,* to His people. But saying that and enacting that in our table fellowship are two different things.

To repeat, the Supper and its practice provide a criterion for measuring and judging the church's faithfulness to the gospel, and, conversely, the New Testament's teaching concerning the gospel provides a criterion for assessing our sacramental life. Jesus frequently described His preaching as an invitation to a feast. Jesus Himself celebrated that feast with tax gatherers and sinners throughout His life and He concinues to celebrate that feast with us in the Eucharist. The gospel thus provides a criterion for judging our admission rules for the table: Is the invitation to the table as wide as the invitation to repent and believe?

We must think about baptism and the Supper in these (overlapping, if not identical) ecclesial and evangelical contexts if we want to grasp what is at stake in the paedocommunion debate. The question is not only who's in and who's out, but also what our decisions about who's in and who's out say about the church we are and the gospel we proclaim. What kind of community are we claiming to be if we invite children to the Lord's table, or, as is more commonly the case, what are we saying about the church when we exclude them? What do our ritual statements about the church say about the church's relation to Israel and the character of salvation? Put our theologies and our sermons to the side for a moment: What gospel does our meal preach?

CHAPTER 2

The New Israel

All paedobaptists agree that the church is the new Israel, formed as the body of the Risen Christ. But paedocommunion reinforces this point dramatically, for it insists that the admission requirements to the church's meal are exactly the same as the admission requirements to Israel's feasts.

Ancient Israel celebrated many different meals with various rules for admission. Some food, classified as "most holy," was reserved exclusively for priests (e.g., Leviticus 24:5–9), and "holy food" could be eaten only by the members of a priestly household (e.g., Leviticus 22:10–16). Both non-priestly adults and their children were excluded from these priestly meals. As priest in the order of Melchizedek, Jesus overcomes the distinction between the priesthood of Aaron and the priesthood of the people of God. As a result, these regulations are no longer directly relevant to the question of admission to the Lord's Supper.

Here's the important point: All Israelites, adults and children, at at all the feasts in Israel's liturgical calendar. Adult males were *required* to participate (Exodus 23:17), but women and children were *allowed* to participate. Children are explicitly invited to participate at the feasts of Pentecost and Booths (Deuteronomy 16:10–14). The central sanctuary was set up for that very purpose, so that Israelites, both parents and children, could celebrate before Yahweh: "And you shall rejoice before Yahweh your God, you and your sons and daughters, your male and female servants, and the Levite who is within your gates, since he has no portion or inheritance with you" (Deuteronomy 12:12). It would be absurd if children were excluded from the feasts of the central sanctuary. That's what the central sanctuary was for.

Though children's inclusion at Passover is never as explicitly stated, there is a compelling—I would say, conclusive—case for paedo-Passover. Exodus 12:3–4 specifies the size of the lamb needed for the meal: "Speak to all the congregation of Israel, saying, "On the tenth of this month they are each one to take a lamb for themselves, according to their fathers' households, a lamb for each household. Now if the household is too small for a lamb, then he and his neighbor nearest to his house are to take one according to the number of souls; according to each man's eating, you are to compute for the lamb."

That is, the Passover lamb had to be at last big enough to feed a household. But what is a "household"? Throughout the Pentateuch, "house" includes children and servants. Noah's "house" obviously included his sons and daughters-in-law (Genesis 7:1), and Abram circumcised his servants as males in his "house" (Genesis 17:23, 27). The very first verse of Exodus tells us that Jacob's sons came to Egypt, each with his "house" (1:1). Nowhere in the Bible does a "household" exclude children. If the lamb was to be large enough for a household, it was to be large enough to give the children of the house a portion. If younger members of the household were not going to eat, why was the size of the lamb large enough to feed them? To taunt them?

Some have suggested the "catechism" of Exodus 12:25–28 shows that children had to be able to answer questions before sharing in the meal. That is a questionable interpretation of the passage, but more importantly, Exodus 12 includes *explicit* instructions about admission to Passover. The chapter ends with the "ordinance" of the Passover, namely, that "no son of a stranger is to eat of it" and that "no uncircumcised person may eat of it" (Exodus 12:43–48). Circumcision is specified as the gateway to Passover. Conversely, those who were excluded from Passover were *ipso facto* being treated as "strangers." Were the young children in Israel "strangers" to the covenant people?

Paul's warning about unworthy participation in the supper (1 Cor. 11:17-34) doesn't affect this argument. Warnings about the dangers of hypocritical participation in the feasts of Israel are common in the prophets (Is. 1:10–17; Jer. 6:20; Amos 5:21–24), yet we know that children participated in these feasts. Could an Israelite celebrate the Feast of Booths in a state of uncleanness? No. Yet children were invited to participate in that meal. If paedocommunion is correct, children of the church are participating in a dangerous meal; but then, God's young children have always participated in dangerous meals.

Antipaedocommunionists sometimes point to the requirement of ritual cleanliness for participation in Passover

(Num. 9), and apply this to the Supper by saying that the participants have to be in a state of spiritual cleanliness. But these rules do not undermine paedocommunion. Under the law, small children would rarely become unclean (Leviticus 12-15). Young girls are never unclean because of menstruation or childbirth, nor have most five-year-old boys ever had a seminal emission or suffered from an STD. They might attend funerals, but they could rapidly be cleansed. Children might love bacon and ham, but if they grew up in ancient Israel they would never have been served these or other unclean meats. To suggest that children were excluded from Passover because of possibility of uncleanness is nonsense.

In the new covenant, these rituals of purification are fulfilled in baptism. And this raises the question of how we should regard our baptized children. In this connection, we might note that the same Paul who warned against unworthy participation in the Supper said in the same letter that the children of believers are "saints" (1 Corinthians 7:14). Dare we call unclean what God has cleansed?

There is a difference between requirements for admission to some privilege and requirements for *proper* use of that privilege. The U.S. Constitution does not require that candidates for Senate be intelligent, honest, self-sacrificing, or righteous. Of course, if he is going to be a *good* Senator, a candidate must be all those things and more. But he is qualified for candidacy by reaching his thirty-fifth year, being a citizen of the United States, and residing in the state in which he is a candidate. Similarly, when Paul exhorts the Corinthians about proper participation in the Supper, he is not giving admission requirements.

Israelite children were permitted to share in every meal in which their parents participated. Because the church is the new Israel, the entry requirements to the church's Passover are the same as they were for Israel. Discontinuity with regard to admission to the table, like discontinuity between the subjects of circumcision and baptism, undermines the identification of the church and Israel. What are we saying about the church when we exclude children from the table? We are saying that we are *not* Israel.

CHAPTER 3

The New Humanity

Paedocommunion not only implies that the church is the new Israel, but that the church is the new humanity. To say the one is to say the other, for Israel was chosen from among the nations to be Yahweh's instrument to reverse the sin at Babel, the sin of the sons of God, the sin of Cain, and the sin of Adam. That reversal only takes place through the faithfulness of the true Israel, Jesus Christ. In Christ, we are called to the same calling as Israel:

to live before the Creator as all mankind was created to live before Him. By maintaining continuity between the rites of Israel and the rites of the church, paedocommunion declares decisively that the church is now the heir to this calling.

The notion that the church is the new humanity rests on fundamental Christological affirmations. In His resurrection Jesus was constituted the "new man," the new Adam (1 Corinthians 15:35-49), and this implies that He is Head of a renewed human race. The same point can be established by a more directly ecclesiological argument. According to Ephesians 2:11-22, the purpose of the cross was to destroy the dividing wall that separated Jew and Gentile, and so to constitute Jew and Gentile into one new humanity. Saying that the church is the new humanity does not mean that every human being is now a member of Christ or His church. But it does mean that nothing human is alien to the church; and, positively, that the life of the church as the community of the New Man encompasses the life of humanity itself. The church is not a "religious" organization in the restricted modern sense; it is a people that, through the power of the Spirit of Jesus, have been converted to and are being discipled in a new way of being human.

Opponents of paedocommunion might well agree with the arguments of the preceding paragraph, but this raises again my initial claim that the rites of the church express the character of the community the church is. Only by including children among the table-fellows of

Christ can the church display with consistency that she is the new human race.

A happy thought experiment will help make the point. Suppose that tomorrow morning we woke up to find every living man and woman, teenager and senior citizen, toddler and infant converted by the Spirit of God, so that we suddenly lived in a world where the human race on earth was made up only of the eternally elect. Suppose too that we were given an incontestable sign that this miracle had occurred, so that there would be no doubt that the human race was thoroughly Christianized.

Under these theoretical circumstances, would the church be coextensive with the now-converted human race? Should Baptists insist on remaining Baptist, the answer would be no. Even under these circumstances, there would be many converted infants and toddlers who could not make what Baptists normally recognize as a credible profession of faith. So, the converted human race would be divided between those who have the capacity to make a profession of faith and those who did not have that capacity. Only the former would be baptized and admitted to the Supper. Even if the whole human race were saved, there would still be a distinction between "church" and "world." Baptists thus imply by their refusal to baptize infants that the church is *not*, even *theoretically*, coextensive with the human race. Believer's baptism implies that the church *is not* the new humanity.

I am sure that many Baptists confess that the church is the new humanity, but there is a rift between confession and sacramental practice. Believer's baptism says of the church that it is not the new humanity, which is also a statement about the character of the gospel. Believer's baptism says of Christ that He is no new Adam, but at best a new Abraham or Moses—the head of a chosen people, but not the head of a new race.

Paedobaptists claim otherwise. If everyone in the world were converted, or if even all the parents of young children were converted, then all would be immediately incorporated into the church by baptism, so that the church would be coextensive with the converted human race. For paedobaptists, the church is by definition the new humanity, and it includes, as the human race itself does, all sorts and conditions of men, all ages and stages of life, all levels of ability and degrees of faith. The church is not an elite religious group for those who can make mature and credible professions. In

Christ, the church is the "one new man." For the paedobaptist, the only thing that excludes a human being from the church is the sin of unbelief. Age, mental or linguistic capacities, and life experience are simply not factors.

But paedobaptist opponents of paedocommunion are inconsistent on this point, and it is an inconsistency that has damaged the witness of paedobaptist churches more deeply than we can fathom. With their rite of baptism, they proclaim that the church is the new human race, theoretically coextensive with mankind as a whole. By making doctrinal knowledge, conversion experience, or some other rite of passage an additional requirement for admission to the Lord's table, however, they take away with bread and wine what they give with water.

On the one hand, they claim that children are initiated into the covenant community, but on the other hand they say that "knowledge" and "spiritual maturity" are required for participation in the meal of the community, the meal that expresses the unity of the community. On the one hand, they say that children of Israel were admitted to Israel by circumcision, but on the other hand, many claim that they were denied the Passover, which was "the sacrament of communion, life and growth." A moment's reflection will reveal the incoherence here: Children are inducted into the church, but denied one of the principal means for growth; they are expected to become mature, but denied one of the key means for attaining maturity. We starve our children, yet bid them, "Be strong!"

But the incoherence of the position is not merely practical. It is ecclesiological and soteriological, Christological and cultural. At the font, paedobaptist opponents of paedocommunion say that grace restores nature; at the table, they say grace has nothing to do with nature. At the font, they say that God's grace can work to make an infant a *saved* infant; at the table, they say that grace begins to restore human life only after one reaches a certain level of maturity. At the font, they say the gospel announces the restoration of the human race; at the table, they say the gospel invites the mature into fellowship with God. At the font, they say the church is the new humanity; at the table, they say the church is a religious community for those who can profess faith. At the font, they proclaim Jesus as the new Adam; at the table, Jesus is 'merely' the new Abraham. At the font, they radically challenge the modern confinement of religion to a circumscribed sphere of life; at the table, they bow to modern assumptions.

In response, an opponent of paedo-communion might say that the infants in the thought experiment are members of the church, but not *communing* members. They are in covenant, but do not participate in this one rite of the covenant. This divides the question: On the one hand, it affirms that the church is the new humanity, but on the other hand, it denies that participation in the church's meal is a necessary privilege of inclusion in that new humanity. I find this inconsistent, but it does reveal an underlying assumption that I must defend, namely, that *inclusion in the covenant meal is a necessary privilege of covenant membership*. I'll address that in the next chapter.

CHAPTER 4

The Privilege of Membership

The thesis here is: Reception of the gifts of baptism an Eucharist is a necessary privilege of membership in the covenant people. There is no covenant membership except one sealed by participation in covenant signs and rites.

I immediately concede any number of qualifications and exceptions to this claim. A baptized and believing woman on life support, for example, cannot receive the elements of the Supper, but is

not thereby cut out of the covenant. But
the refusal to admit infants or toddlers
to the table is an entirely different sort
of refusal. The woman does not participate in the meal because she is physical-
ly incapable of doing so. From a fairly
young age, however, children are capable
of receiving the elements, but are refused
admission to the table until they can
display appropriate mental, spiritual, or
emotional responses. Their exclusion is
based on principle, while the woman's
exclusion is contingent on circumstances
beyond her control.

One of the fundamental issues at
stake in the paedocommunion debate
has to do with the nature of covenant.
Though distinctions between the "form"
and the "substance" of the covenant are
quite traditional, they are highly mis-
leading. Scripturally, the term *covenant*

describes both God's self-commitment to His people and the set of prescribed practices, laws, and rites—the whole pattern of life and worship revealed by God and by which we live before Him. Keeping covenant, for the Israelite, meant following the statutes, ordinances, laws, and practices that Yahweh revealed to Israel; breaking covenant meant turning aside from this way of life (see Leviticus 26:14–15; Deuteronomy 29:1; Hebrews 9:1–10).

Just as there is no marriage covenant without an exchange of vows (normally public, at least before a justice of the peace), and no continuing marital relationship except through through sexual and other forms of bodily communion, so there simply is no covenant where there are no external forms. The covenant is not some invisible reality *behind* the forms. The visible, ritual, practical forms are constituent elements of covenant.

This visible pattern of worship and life is of the essence of the covenant because the covenant is a communal reality. God entered into covenant with Abraham, but the Abrahamic covenant embraced his household and future generations. In later covenants, the corporate character is even more evident, as Yahweh makes and renews His covenant with Israel. God established the pattern of life for the public community of Israel, a covenantal order revealed by God and encompassing Israel's worship, politics and civil justice, family life, and every other aspect of their life as a people. Being corporate, the covenant necessarily takes external and ritual form, for, as theologians from Augustine to Aquinas and beyond recognized, no community can function as a community without some public expression of its communion.

To speak of Israel's covenant is to speak of Israel's divinely-ordained "cultural" order, and to speak of a new covenant is to speak of a new "cultural" order in the church. Participation in the covenant necessarily means participation in the practices of the covenant, for there is no other kind of participation in the covenant, because there is no other kind of covenant. Denying that participation in covenant rites is essential to covenant membership is inherently Baptistic, even if the denial comes from paedobaptists.

Opponents of paedocommunion argue that children receive the blessings of the covenant without the sign. Baptists say the very same thing about baptism. Here is the dilemma: Why does covenant membership without the sign suffice for the Supper but not for baptism? Why must admission to the covenant community take ritual form, but not the continuing membership in the covenant community?

Of course, I am assuming that participation in the Supper is an important, if not the only, public indicator of continuing membership in the church. In the Bible, the covenantal pattern by which the church lives centers on worship. In a number of places, Paul characterizes the "Gentiles" as essentially idolaters and describes conversion as a turning from idols to worship of the living God (e.g., Romans 1:18–23; 1 Thessalonians 1:9; Galatians 4:1–11). As Peter says, we have been constituted as a holy priesthood to offer spiritual sacrifices to God in Christ (1 Peter 2:1–10).

Mission is essential to the life of the church, but mission aims at gathering worshipers before the throne of God. Worship is thus the *telos* of the church in a way that mission is not and cannot be, for when mission is done, there will yet remain worship and love. To participate in the new humanity that is the church, then, means to participate in worship. If one does not participate in the worship of the church, he is simply not a member of the covenant community (see Hebrews 10:25).

Worship, the chief practice of the new humanity, takes place at the Lord's table. It always has. From the time of Abel, worshipers have gathered at the Lord's table/altar. In the Bible, the altar is Yahweh's table (Ezekiel 44:16), where His "bread" was offered in smoke to Him (see Leviticus 22:17, 21), and from which His people received portions (e.g., Leviticus 7:11-18). For Paul, "coming together to eat" was synonymous with "coming together" (1 Corinthians 11:17, 18, 33). Skeptics on Mars Hill heard the word of the gospel, but they were not thereby part of a covenant people or involved in a liturgical act. Proclamation or teaching of the Word is an inherent part of worship, but that is not what defines worship as worship. The church worships when it gathers at the Lord's table.

If the covenant *is* the form of communal life, if membership in the covenant involves participation in the external practices and rites of the covenant, if worship is the central practice of the new covenant people, and if worship centers on a meal with God, then participation in the covenant meal is a necessary privilege of being in covenant. If baptized infants really are in covenant with God, they should participate in the meal of that covenant. If they are in the body symbolized by the loaf, can we withhold the loaf from them? And if they are not really in covenant with God, then why in God's name do we continue to baptize them?

CHAPTER 5

Conclusion

The sacraments should, I have argued, reflect the character of the church. More fundamentally, they should reflect the character of the gospel by which the church has been gathered and in whose power she lives. Though the gospel is not directly implicated in the paedocommunion debate, it is close to the heart of the issues. Opponents of paedocommunion turn the Supper into an act that requires spiritual maturity, reversing the basic meaning of the Supper and ritually denying the nature of the church and the Reformation *solas*.

The Protestant tendency to restrict the evangelical invitation to God's table to the spiritually accomplished has done as much to undermine the pure gospel of grace as a hundred Papal bulls and a dozen Tridentine councils. We can shout the formulas until we are hoarse, but still our actions will shout down our words. If the Reformed churches hope to advance the gospel with power in our day, we must ensure that our central liturgical act is brought into conformity to the gospel.